A GIRL WITH KALEIDOSCOPE EYES

A GIRL WITH KALEIDOSCOPE EYES
copyright © 2023 by Niya Appana. All rights reserved.
Printed in the United States of America. No portion of this book may
be used or reproduced in any form without written permission from
the author, except as permitted by U.S. copyright law or in the case
of reprints for reviews.

Cover Art: Anastasiia Dzhioeva

Illustrations: Niya Appana, Amara Appana,
and Genesis Gomez

Table of Contents

Is this better than a text message?

A GIRL WITH KALEIDOSCOPE EYES[1]

Niya Appana

<hr>

[1]"Lucy in the Sky with Diamonds" by The Beatles (1967)

This work is a product of the author's recollection of certain events, circumstances, and conversations. In order to maintain discretion, identifying characteristics of such may have been altered or avoided.

The following material includes themes of several mental illnesses. Please be advised that its contents may not be suitable for some audiences.

If you or someone you know is struggling with a mental illness, you are not alone. For general information on mental health and to identify resources available in your region, consult SAMHSA.gov or call SAMHSA's National Helpline at 1-800-662-HELP.

FROM THE AUTHOR

This book is a love letter to every good and bad thing that has ever happened to me. I never thought I could do this, let alone finish it and allow people to read it. But what is there to follow creation than reception?

None of this would've been possible without my family. To Amara (and by proxy Iko) and Ericka, my sisters and two-thirds of my soul, I would've given up a long time ago if not for you. To my mom, the strongest force of nature, you gave me everything I've ever needed in my life and more. It wasn't my own luck to be blessed with good hands, you gave them to me. These are my words but this book is our voices.

To every new home we stepped foot in. To all the miles we've lived apart. To every hospital waiting room, every cancer center, every funeral, everyone and everything we lost on the way.

To everyone who has ever made an impact on my life and changed the way I think about myself, others, and the world, thank you for showing me differently.

Perhaps the biggest thank you to my medical leave from university and insomnia for forcing me to finish this from my mom's couch.

Here's to illness, to loss, to change, to everyone who has ever loved me (and even everyone who has ever hurt me), to my family, to me—and to you.

Poetry is written with love and is meant to be read with love. The interpretation of art varies from person to person, so as you read this collection, I only ask you to keep one thing in mind: it's all in the eyes.

Niya Appana

"Look for the girl with the sun in her eyes and she's gone"

Because I'm a writer I like to pretend I'm happy when I write about a world where birds look more alive and paved roads wave like the ocean and kiwis are universally recognized as sweet fruits instead of sour when really the world is made up of owners dragging their dogs against hot concrete in a park named after someone lost to history and humans cutting down trees to put up apartment buildings we decorate with greenery and at some point we realize we live in a dollhouse of a world where institutions have designed us to fail as a society but we've progressed too far to dismantle these institutions

Because I'm a writer I don't like when people tell me that words are empty and they're not real and actions speak louder because if actions speak louder what do writers speak up for? To act is to perform and I don't want to perform even though that's exactly what I do when I write about a world where people spread love and appearance equates to less than color and we all pretend we weren't the ones who ruined the world and instead it's just the temperament of nature because it sounds nice but it's not real

But I always believed when I put words down they became real?

Trying to translate the world around us into a world we would actually want to live in because we desire a nature not man-made so we man-make it.

The world in itself categorized
by both its beauty
and its
h
y
p
o
c
r
i
s
y

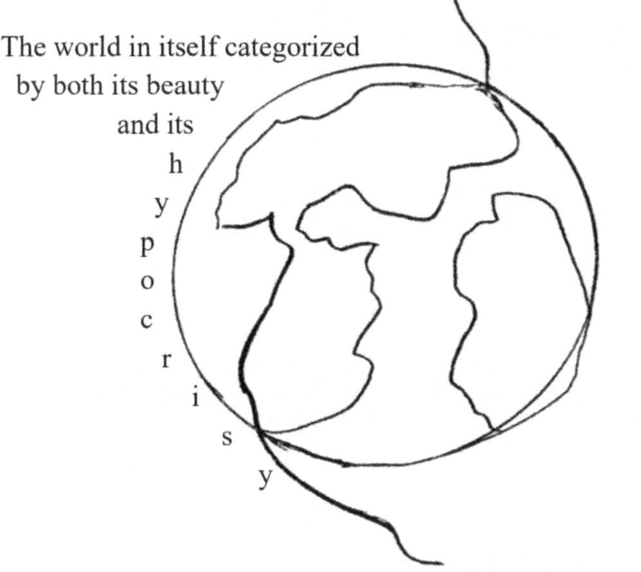

If someone asked me about you, I don't know what I would say...

Would I start with a physical description? Would I spew off some rehearsed-sounding list of relatively positive adjectives, not too interpersonal, but personal enough for people to believe that I actually knew you?

Or, maybe in trying to answer that question, I think I would have to first talk about myself. Or I guess, I just would.

I would start with a preface like everyone with a need to overcompensate and overexplain and overdramatize would do. And I would do it because I am someone with a need to overcompensate and overexplain and overdramatize.

The thing is I don't know what I'm overcompensating for and to whom I'm overexplaining and why I'm overdramatizing… but awareness and intention sometimes don't coexist and inform one another. Instead, sometimes they take bites out of each other until you're left with something that starts a lot like this.

You were funny. The type of funny that everyone definitely wouldn't find funny but since I did, you were funny. You remind me of my dad in that way. He doesn't tell too many jokes but he's still funny. Ironically, he's a man of very few words (a trait you would've benefited from). But when he uses those very few words, the way he uses them is… funny. This is mostly because he talks to amuse himself, audience be damned. One of his most notable characteristics is his ability to laugh in your face. Laughing in your face because he found you funny. Not by the jokes you would tell or by your quirky behavior, but by the way you would never be funny like him. Maybe we're not still talking about the word funny.

You were kind. Not the going-out-of-your-way-for- random-strangers type of kind but somewhat adjacent. You would've done anything for me, not for just anyone, but definitely for me. You remind me of my mom in that way. She used to do everything for everyone and now she would only do anything for me. The thing about being kind is that genuinely kind people don't look for a reward or at least admit that's what they're hoping for. When you constantly go out of your way for people (not including random strangers) and you receive no reward, you start viewing giving as losing. I think at some point she realized that kindness was not being rewarded and she was constantly losing. The cost of being "kind" I suppose.

I'm not really sure if she's still a kind person.

I'm not.

untitled

Velvet sweet crisp how I like my wine
Brown and bitter how I like my rum
I was never much of a drinker but you know what they say about
love

Blind leading the blind

I think I remember what happened last night
or at least that's what you said
I believe you more than I believe what's in my head

So if you call me the worst person you've ever met
I will believe you
And if you tell me I'm no better than the people who have hurt you
I will believe you

Because you know me better than anyone,
I'm a liar and I love everyone.

They're all the same and so am I

He's not like the other guys he's funny and he makes me laugh not like my ex-boyfriend who did not have a single funny bone in his body and not like the other ones who didn't have enough sense in their heads to think I was funny or to think I was smart or to think… well now that I think about it I guess they never did think much of me but I guess that's what makes him different because he cares about what I think and who I am and what I find funny but I'm worried it won't be enough and I'll get tired of him

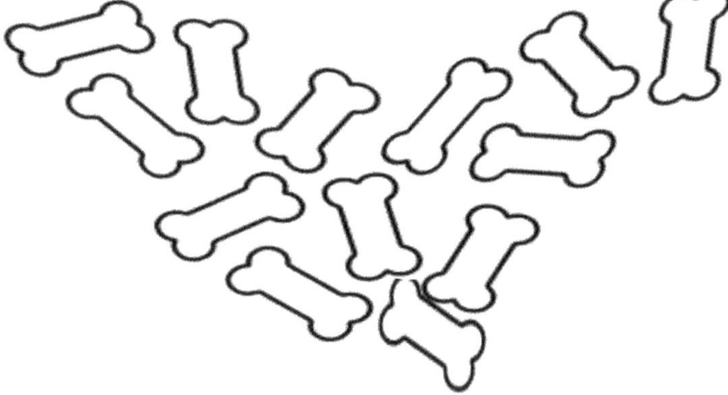

sure he's funny but funny can get repetitive and then funny gets boring and then sometimes funny can equal *friendly* and I wonder if other girls find him funny and therefore find him *friendly* which I hate the thought of but how can I be jealous over someone whose funniness gives me pause because if funny gets boring I know how I can be when I get bored and it's probably just because I'm an insatiable person and wonder if I'll be a cheater like my dad because I always seem to find things so unfulfilling and
…funny?

paranoia

silhouette in the doorway
shadow on the stairs
the tongue uncomfortably sits in the mouth when you notice it
i never stop noticing you

look at me through the holes of visual transparencies
instead of the mouth
seize the words from my throat

until the only sentences i am capable of
producing are the ones you seem to
have forgotten

I'll remind you
and everyone.

I'm afraid of the ocean

My eyes are black and beady and there's no depth at least not at the first impression so I always thought you had a unique ability to look into the soul since the eyes are the windows to the soul because into my soul is the only place you would see a color I never wear and the image of a place I never go because I'm afraid of its contents similar to how I was afraid for you to see me for the first time since I had a feeling you would look deeper than you were supposed to and would wade right through the massive shallow I believe to comprise my aura and see that I am all the things I am disturbed by and made up of all the things I'm uncomfortable with and deep down I am even the things that I deny about both myself and you.

When you look so deeply it makes it hard for me to be the person I think you're looking for, which is something I'm going to have to keep in mind for next time. Or for the next person.

Alphabet City

Electricity ran in my elated elastic
Evade me and I e   r   u   p   t
Elusive and enchanting
                                 endowing your ego ^{elevated} mine
The eager eagle earns what he unearths

I always desired the dark delicacy
                    you to delve into me
Your deadly daze could not deter me
I was drafted by your   dancing   divinity

Cataclysm continued and caught in
a clock between   our closure
Clarity captured in clusters of contrition
Could it be concealed by calamity
Or can I coexist in your chaos?

My boy beloved blatant and brash
Blood of my backbone begging for battle
You   breached   the   balance
                of   my   blackjack

Alas I could be awoken
Asserting your ambrosia to my alignment

Against
my
ability
to
alliterate

The antagonist

His lack of companion and my limit in perception,
I know he does not exist in the way I write him

but that is the way I must tell you the story because he had a spirit
unlike the rest of us.

And I must be morally superior for sympathy,
        just not better than you would believe me to be.

I'm sorry you met me

If I could fly
If I could turn back time
Maybe I wouldn't feel nothing
I could go back to the day we met
I could tell him
I can't be who you want
I could tell him
If I could fly
If maybe you'd seen the way I cry
If maybe you'd seen me through our goodbyes
You'd see the me behind my eyes

And if you could remember what you'd seen,
                 you would feel nothing.

I've convinced myself of many things

indifference is bliss

I'm not complex
I'm difficult

anything is better than nothing

they likely are
right about me

my ignorance will come to fruition

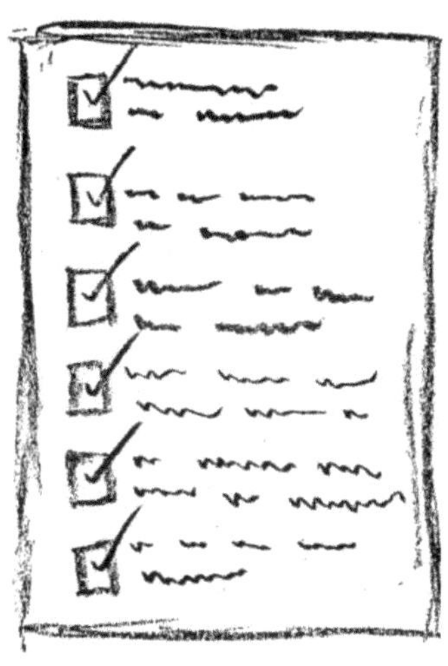

I am just being *difficult*

<u>This is not a love poem</u>

I don't like to write poems about people
I worry I'll get carried away

I wanted to try this once
Could I make you mean more?
More than only something to me?

So I tried to write about you…

To write you out of my life and into others
To reduce you to my words and into a lover
To give your name a home
To make you into a beautiful poem

But the poem was bland and I broke the pen in my hand.

A poem I can control
and you,

    are you.

Ferryman

Eat my heart out before you dissect my brain
Glutton is my pleasure and pleasure is pain

Make sure to put coins over my eyes
I heard that keeps people safe

Purposefully I adorn myself in gold
I pray it will lead me to the same fate

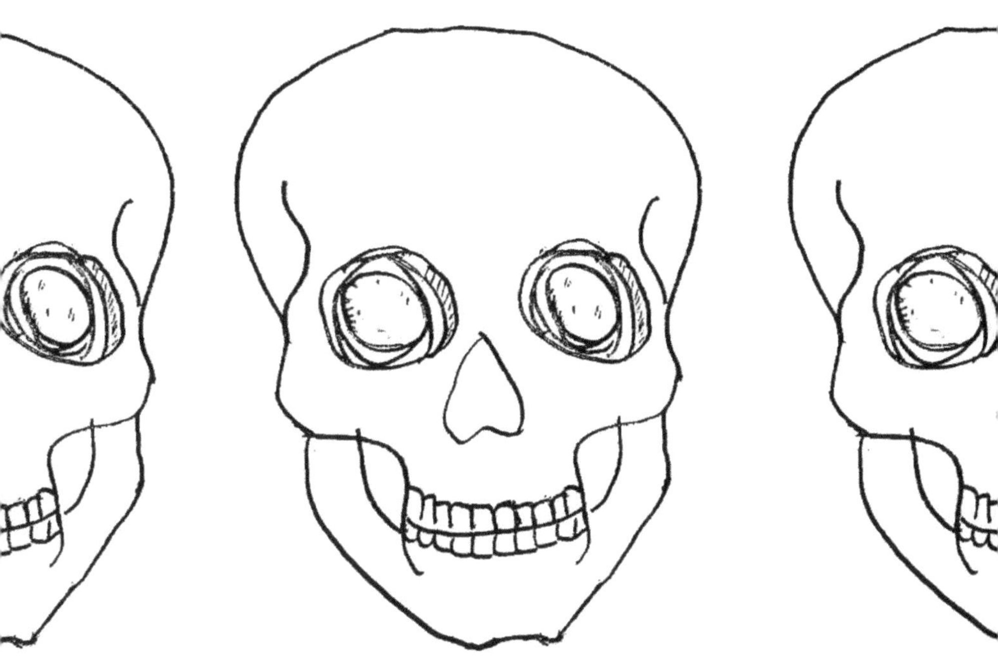

you didn't really know me and neither do i

i made myself into a bird

                                        tugged on by gravity

tired of soaring into self-prescribed tragedy

                                                 I tried

instead i dove headfirst into the sabotage of the sun's rays

                                  no grace in my flight
                                  no mercy in my beak

i didn't like who you were when you were mad at me

                                  what else should I be?

i took shelter in those rays
to burn away the etching of your talons on my skin
pretending it wasn't too late

I could've flown past you

maybe then i would flinch less at the memories
the cloud of regretful nostalgia within my mind's reach
i didn't possess the ability to remove myself from it

so I couldn't be me.

i was the bird until i wasn't
i tried to make him understand but he just doesn't

he doesn't even think of me when he looks at the sky
it's my fault for thinking he could know me when really
                              neither do I.

An artist is always alone *(if she is an artist)*

I ruined a drawing once trying to erase all of my mistakes. I'm afraid I don't know what art is.

I'm on the last chapter of a book you haven't even started

You were right to say it. I don't read, I create. I leave whatever words I want to in my wake but not a word you say to me will ever resonate because I don't open the books you read and I don't read the books you write and if you didn't like my writing I never really cared because writing is the tool I use to prepare to control my fears and you assumed if I was never writing about you then what exactly is it that I hold dear? But the answer to that question will never be written because my words are masks and what is dear is unwritten.

67

I resolve, I resign

Mercifully   magically   masterfully
make a mess of me

Is this acceptance or is this my submission?

For reckless is the resignation to redundancy,
as true indulgence remains both imprudent

                    and triumphant.

until I stop wondering

I found it scary how often I wondered what if

how my mind wandered to other relationships that felt more like home
   who i would be without you and that the answer was likely a better person
      where i would be if i wasn't afraid to explore and that it would probably be a better place
         why i wanted more when happiness was in reach and expected more when it wasn't
            about the times in my life when i was less than satisfied but at least i felt an emotion

It made me wonder if I am later in my story than I think

> and i wondered who else would settle
> for perishable goods but me
> and i wondered how much damage i
> left in my wake
> and i wondered if my issues started
> yours
> and i wondered if my choices in life
> were what led me astray
> and i wondered if they would be
> disappointed in how much i disappoint
> myself
> and i wondered if i could go back to the
> person i was before
> and i wondered what my life would be
> like if i had truly healed except I haven't

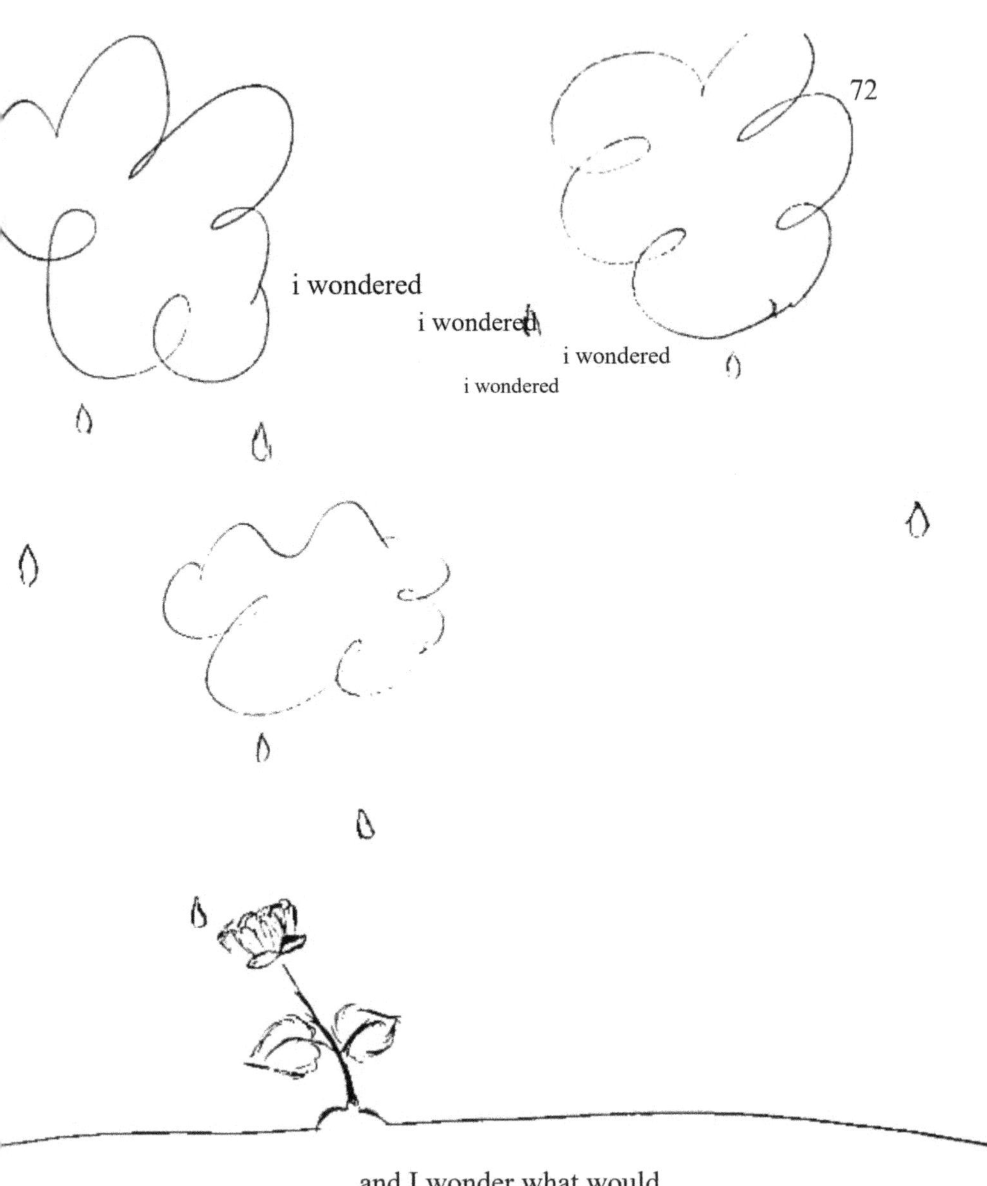

and I wonder what would
happen if i stopped wondering.

Throw a wish in the wishing well

I wish the world was 2d
little dimensional portals shaped like squares are all
it would take to reach me

When I looked at the sky, it didn't seem so far
but the longer I looked, the less I believe we're really
seeing the stars

Maybe if I could see things differently, I would trust the people
telling me the world is immense and great
I can't see past the idea that I see things incorrectly
                    I have an immovable fate

All these years to move on I thought only required distance and
space
but I don't think I could ever put into words the significance of time
and place.

Brain fog

Somewhere in my memory loss I began to figure people just take take and take and they tell you they relate and good memories are yours to make but before I can make any of those of my own I simply can't concentrate and how can I take their advice when I don't remember whose advice to take or what advice was a mistake when it's from people who don't know what's at stake so I don't remember when I stopped believing every day would be great and I don't remember when I realized there were some feelings I couldn't shake and I don't remember when I learned not just my bones but my organs would break because people like me are always awake and we wait for the moments where the weight of the noise subsides and the fire around the house I reside that is controlled by my pride all seem to coincide when inanimate structures confide in me but

I don't remember what they say about the eyes and the lines and the signs because forgetfulness was the first feeling I couldn't shake and waiting around at night for peace of mind are the times I feel my heart break and if my memory would only serve me right which it never does I would remember why I stopped believing and started realizing every day can't be great

3...2...1

Days evade and pass me by like a countdown
I turned around three times, where did she go?
Am I alone?
When I look in the mirror I see two of me
She answers my questions sometimes
If only I had asked how many days until a better
one

I had a dream

My eyes cannot betray me when I'm asleep
I'm not hallucinating I'm having a dream

I'm having a dream when I see those people who are my friends
I don't think my mind would give me enemies

Enemies of the mind are the enemies of me
Except I have no enemy who looks different than me

Once upon a time

Insects lay on my knee
        crushing weeds in my shoes
Joint with the earth,
        I am me
                I am you

Swirls of green in the sky I've never seen
I remember Jack, is this his stalk of bean?

What grows besides the ego with force,
A children's fable my own dark horse

The magic went with the wind,
the tulip's sun whispered to a dim
Folk tales I search for remain only
        under my skin

A caterpillar sings for a garden uprooted,
and dances in rain falling to
a world polluted.

I'm getting dizzy

I looked at the world and everything seemed so still

Am I the only with the gift of stand-still sight
Did the world stop moving or
did I

                    I wish I could stop moving

By stop moving I don't mean stop breathing excuse

my intrusive thoughts when she says the things you **I**
don't like to hear

I mean stay in place I mean hit the pause button I
mean hold a steel barrier to time and tell him that I
will not budge until I am ready
I mean

stop moving.

I'm sorry I met you

If you were like me
the founder of indifference
we could've reinvented memory

Instead
seared into my brain is a disdain for fantasy
veiled compulsion I don't usually notice
against my better nature   my inability to focus

And if only I would remember what you do to me,
I would feel nothing.

At least we are under the same sky...

One day when you finally come to the city I dreamed
of showing you,
I hope you don't think of me.

I actually hope you've forgotten all about me.

I hope this place is exactly what you thought
it would be and I hope you're in the place
I always thought you would be
And mostly I hope if you pass me
on the street, you don't notice me

I know I'll be missing you
because I already do.

We wouldn't be in
different places if only
you'd miss me too.

Me vs them

I am so resentful to hear they are well
(no I don't care but if I did, can you tell?)

I can't help that feeling of bitterness creep
their new linens and my stained sheets
their laughs of glory and my silent weep
I'm always awake and they're always asleep?

As their words flow to my ears, I wonder which part of my brain
controls sound and which part can block it out.

I wonder what they wonder about.

I'm so inspired by you

Are you proud of how far I've taken my writing?
Are you happy to be my muse?

> (Would you still be proud of me
> knowing I'm lying to you?)

I'll be honest
I racked my brain for a sonnet
I paced my room for a rhyme
I couldn't find the words

> (not because you left me speechless
> but because you made my writing worse)

I spent hours trying to write the things we both had already known,
but apparently I can't write love poems until I know where this
goes…

Though
I wish I could've done it for you

I know I am better on my own.

The writer's paradox

My favorite things to write are those that no one will
ever read
I'm a control freak and I can't control which parts of
me people will perceive

My favorite pieces of writing I keep to myself
I'm selfish and I want praise for my words but not for them to live
on your shelf

I keep my writing lonely because I'm actually afraid,
No one who has read my favorites has ever stayed.

Forgot my happy pills

When I hear thumping in my ear and realize it's the
beating of my heart
I remember that I need to breathe if I want the
volume to reduce
I remember my throat feels tighter when my own
trapped air surrounds my neck like a noose
                    and I *do* remember but what's the use?

Everything I do to me, I do through you

Except you don't feel my pain
in fact my pain lies around your neck a beautiful chain

You know how to breathe
The words flow from your throat with ease
I hear a haunting thump
You hear a blissful melody
How can I be your company and you my enemy?

To share a body and never be at peace,

everything I do for you
I
happen
to
be
doing
to
me

Trigger warning?

I would never harm a soul except my own. My pain is self–inflicted and self-restricted because I feel what I desire and preserve what I wish to be rid of and I don't like to destroy the memories of the color in my eyes and ache in my heel when I pass through concrete and fall floor to floor trying to find ways to allow the cement to reshape my lungs into hardness and my body into wholeness and my mind into quietness.

The soul is a quiet place and I would never
intentionally bring it harm,
except my soul does not belong to me and I don't
believe in self-harm.

Patience is a virtue

While I wait for this quick fix
                                    for this instant relief
for this ability to tell reality from my dreams
I both laugh   and cry
I sabotage   then sigh
I keep you a safe distance away because I must shield you
from what you don't know is inside
In me is a battle

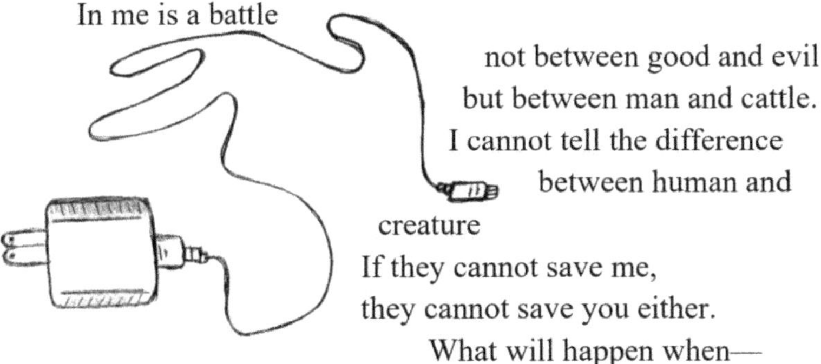

                    not between good and evil
                    but between man and cattle.
                    I cannot tell the difference
                        between human and
        creature
If they cannot save me,
they cannot save you either.
                    What will happen when—
Oh! What a funny feeling. Quiet. Now I have to fix
  the life I don't remember why I ruined.

I am me

Finally I see myself through a different sky through
another lie through my third eye but the eyes don't
see what the mind can make up and the mind can't
make up the thoughts from when I wake up   the
images in my dreams only time can shape up because if I am me then
who are you and if you're in my head and you're the seam that I
thread and the stitches that I mend when I play pretend and you tell
me we are friends and what life will look like for me if I only
transcend…   I think about how maybe time bends and twists and
writhes and shatters other things before it shatters my mind but I
worry I'd quicker shatter my mind than my hands because I am me
and I'm the only one who can make you understand

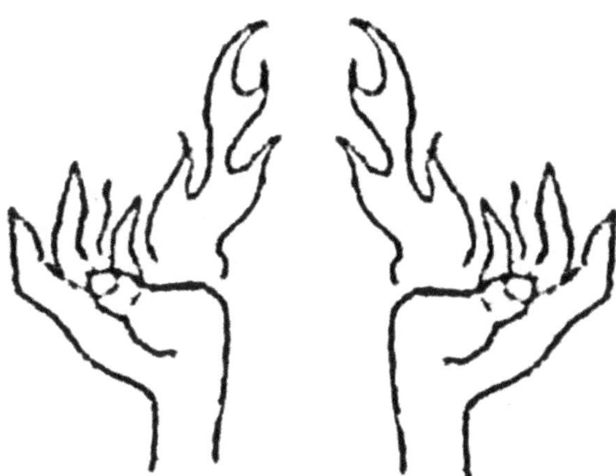

I would love to believe in certain things without feeling stupid.
Like believing that somewhere in the world someone is thinking of you.
You crossed their mind as they went about their day but it was fleeting, you think.
Maybe they dreamt of you the night before.
Maybe they listened to *that* song and remembered your terrible singing.
Maybe they heard someone say something in the way you always used to and they thought of the first and last times they heard you say it.
Then other times, for no reason, you just happen to cross their mind.
No reason, no reminder.

They think they're stupid for still thinking of you without a reason and you think they have no reason to think of you so you feel stupid too.

And so maybe the biggest enemy of thought is reason. Or the feeling of stupidity.

Back & Forth

When I wake up in the morning, holding my
toothbrush at an angle I brush
back & forth

As the paste glides across my teeth, I think about
how last night I couldn't sleep and spent my time
tossing
back & forth

When I was a kid, it was the same routine every morning, deciding
what colors to wear and thinking about how I overheard my parents
last night yelling
                              back & forth

After I would rush downstairs, afraid of being alone
for too long, I would walk into the kitchen seeing the
same scene of my mom buttering my toast, gliding
the knife
                              back & forth

I was always early to school unlike any of my friends
and unlike everyone else, so I would feel a little lonely
walking through the halls
>
> back & forth

And when I would sit in class stuck in the world in
my head, I would write stories on wide-ruled paper
moving my number 2 pencil
>
> back & forth

And when I found myself feeling less than inspired
and comfortless, I would sit behind that school desk
tapping my foot
>
> back & forth

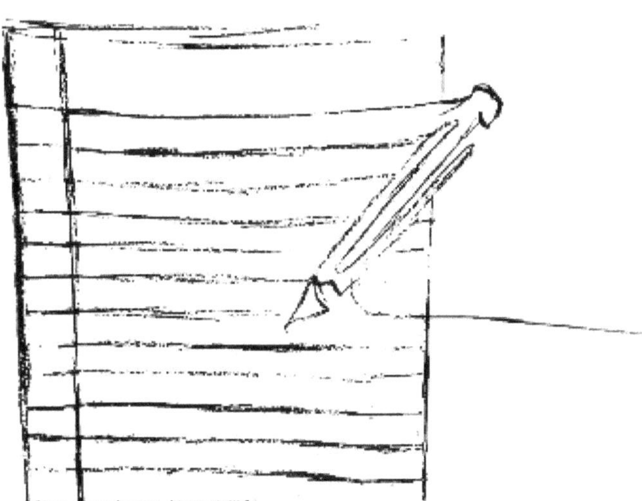

The older I got and the more that I thought, I found myself always
going back

                        and never moving forth.

I noticed that the people who mistreated me always seemed to be
ahead of me. They turned their backs and I never moved forth.

But when I would forget that mistreatment and
re-enter the same situations, it didn't feel like going
back and forth

                              I convinced myself
                  all movement was movement forth.

Going back to
the people
the feelings
the circumstances
that made me uncomfortable

They asked me to turn my back to what made me uncomfortable
and I did.

I asked to turn my back on myself and *I did*.

How could I move forth?

I lost my spine,
I was backless.
Nothing holding me up
anymore
to move

no more back,
no more forth.

Stuck in these moments of immobility, there's a distant memory of the movement I once knew to do…

I try to find power in the movement of myself
                                    back & forth
and I try to forget everything and everyone else who
has made me go
                                    back & forth
and I try to remember when I was younger and back & forth was
reserved for stories and buttered bread and teeth.

every time I wake up in the morning
I am reminded to move

even if it's   *back & forth.*

Stating the obvious so I don't forget

The sky is blue
I could be happier if I tried
Winter is cold
I'm happier when it's cold
All feelings are fleeting
I don't always have to be happy

A half glass of water
is neither half full
nor half empty.

Curiosity killed the cat but satisfaction…

So I want to ask if you still think I'm a bad person. If you think my existence is a manufacturer's flaw. If the stars aren't twinkling but blinking. If the sun hides every time I'm not looking. If the line between good and evil can be patrolled. Why games like tic-tac-toe were fun as kids but not anymore. If God sort of feels that way every time he watches our lives amount to a game of Xs and Os (full of love, sorrow, and wonder, but over quickly). If you are upset that I won't say your name. If now you see,

we are actually the same.

A GIRL WITH KALEIDOSCOPE EYES

Because I'm a writer I like to write about situations that aren't real and people that aren't real and perspectives that are possible but not real and feelings that just don't have fitting words to describe them but I use those mediocre words anyways because words aren't real and I don't like what's real so I like to write about how much you love me and how much control I have over my life and about a world where the only important things are how vibrant certain shades of blue are and how walking with less weight in your step means you're a happier person and how the world's saturation changes based on your mood and how I think I inherited negativity because I only just yesterday noticed how the sky is different every day and none of those things make sense but since I believe in writing things into existence I will continue to

After all… what is there to follow creation than reception?